W9-DFA-391

iScience
Readers

Fabric:
It's Got You Covered!

by Emily Sohn and Lisa Klobuchar

Chief Content Consultant
Edward Rock
Associate Executive Director, National Science Teachers Association

NORWOOD HOUSE PRESS
Chicago, IL

Norwood House Press
PO Box 316598
Chicago, IL 60631

For information regarding Norwood House Press, please visit our website at
www.norwoodhousepress.com or call 866-565-2900.

Special thanks to: Amanda Jones, Amy Karasick, Alanna Mertens, Terrence Young, Jr.

Editors: Barbara J. Foster, Diane Hinckley
Designer: Daniel M. Greene
Production Management: Victory Productions, Inc.

Library of Congress Cataloging-in-Publication data

Sohn, Emily.

Fabric: it's got you covered! / by Emily Sohn and Lisa Klobuchar;
chief content consultant, Edward Rock.

p. cm.

Summary: "Describes the different fabrics we use for clothes: where they
come from, how they're made, and when it's best to use them. As readers use
scientific inquiry to learn how to tell which fabric to use and why, an activity
based on real world situations challenges them to apply what they've learned
in order to solve a puzzle"—Provided by publisher.

Includes bibliographical references and index.

ISBN-13: 978-1-59953-406-0 (lib. ed.: alk. paper)
ISBN-10: 1-59953-406-1 (lib. ed.: alk. paper)

1. Textile fabrics—Juvenile literature. 2. Clothing and dress—Juvenile literature.
I. Klobuchar, Lisa. II. Title.

TS1446.S64 2011
677—dc22
2010044546

••

Manufactured in the United States of America in North Mankato, Minnesota.

173R—022011

Contents

Note to Caregivers:

Throughout this book, many questions are posed to the reader. Some are open-ended and ask what the reader thinks. Discuss these questions with your child and guide him or her in thinking through the possible answers and outcomes. There are also questions posed which have a specific answer. Encourage your child to read through the text to determine the correct answer. Most importantly, encourage answers grounded in reality while also allowing imaginations to soar. Information to help support you as you share the book with your child is provided in the back in the **Additional Notes** section.

Words that are **bolded** are defined in the glossary in the back of the book.

What Are They Wearing?

Go to a busy place and look at people. What kind of clothes do you see? You might see shirts, pants, and skirts. You might see sweaters, socks, and ties. Some people wear lots of colors. Some do not. But everyone wears clothes.

In this book, you will learn about **fabrics.** That's what clothes are made of. You will also solve a fabric puzzle.

What to Wear?

You are going camping with your friends. You will carry all of your clothes in a backpack. It might be hot or cold. It might be sunny or rainy. It might even snow!

Clothes are made of fabric.

There are many kinds of fabric.

What kind of clothes should you pack for the trip?

Here are four ideas for what your clothes should be made of:

Fabric 1: Cotton

Fabric 3: Silk

Fabric 2: Wool

Fabric 4: Polyester

Which fabric will keep you most comfortable when it gets hot, cold, or wet outside?

Discover Activity

Which Fabric Lets in Water?

Most jeans are made of cotton. Sweaters might be **wool.** Scarves may be **silk.** You might find a **polyester** jacket. Read labels on the clothes. Labels can tell you a lot.

You can learn a lot about your clothes from their labels.

Get an adult to help you.

Gather a few examples of fabric, such as old clothing or rags.

Put them flat on a desk or a table.

Pour a little water on the cotton fabric with a spoon.

Did the water soak in? Or did it drip off?

silk fabric

Now pour some water on the other fabrics.

(Remember—just ask an adult first!)

Which ones soak up the water and get really wet?

Do drops form on any of the fabrics? Do any of the fabrics stay dry?

How Is Fabric Made?

Farmers use special cutters, called shears, to get the hair off sheep.

It's not easy to make fabric.
The first step is to find **fibers.**
These are tiny threads.

Some fibers come from nature.
Wool is made from the hair of sheep. People shave the wool off the animals. Silk is made by caterpillars!

Can you think of other animal hair that can become fabric?

Flax plants have purple flowers.

raw cotton

Some fibers come from plants. Cotton plants have fibers. The fibers surround the plant's seeds. **Flax** plants have fibers. The fibers come from the plant's stems. People have to pull fibers off plants and sort them. The fabric made from flax fibers is called linen.

Some fibers, such as the ones in your windbreaker, are made by people. These are called **synthetic** fibers. They don't come from animals or plants.

Are most of your clothes from animal, plant, or synthetic fibers?

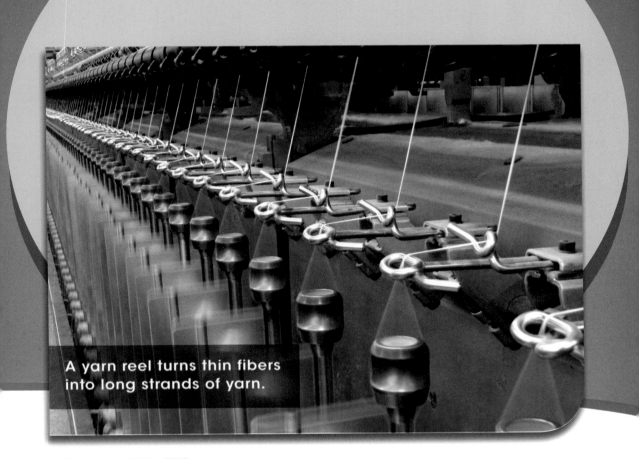

A yarn reel turns thin fibers into long strands of yarn.

Dizzy with Fibers

Machines twist fibers together. This process is called spinning. Spinning makes fibers long and strong. The result is called **yarn.**

You arrive at the campground. It is getting cold. Do you want to wear clothes made out of thick yarn or thin yarn?

little wheel, or pulley

big wheel, or fly wheel

The spinner turns the big wheel with her feet. The little wheel turns and twists fibers into yarn.

Connecting to History

Spinning on a Wheel

Today, you can buy yarn and fabric in stores. Long ago, people made everything by hand. The first spinning wheels were used in China during the mid 1200s. At first, they used their fingers to twist fibers together. Later, they held a tool called a spindle in one hand and another tool, called a distaff, in the other. Still later, they used spinning wheels to help. Some people still spin fibers this way!

The Final Product

The next step is to **weave** yarn into fabric. Strings of yarn cross over and under each other. The strings that go one way are called the warp. The strings that go the other way are called the weft.

Can you see the warp and weft in this fabric?

Knitting is done in many patterns. How many patterns can you find in this sweater?

Knitting is another way to turn yarn into fabric. Little knots hold the yarn together. Knit fabrics have tiny holes. The holes let air and water through.

What Are Some Kinds of Fabric?

Night falls on the campsite. It is getting cold. Which fabric is best now?

Wool keeps sheep warm. How does it do that? It holds warm air in. It keeps cool air out.

Some socks are made of wool.

Most T-shirts are made of cotton.

Cotton fabrics can be thin or thick. But all cotton fibers let air through.

Synthetic fibers are made to be like natural fibers. They can help keep you either warm or cool.

Should you wear the same fabrics during the hot day and the cold night? Which might be better at each time of day?

moth

cocoon

silkworm

Silk is very soft. It is warm. It is also very thin and light. That makes it easy to carry in a backpack.

When might silk be better than wool? When would wool be better?

Getting Wet, Staying Dry

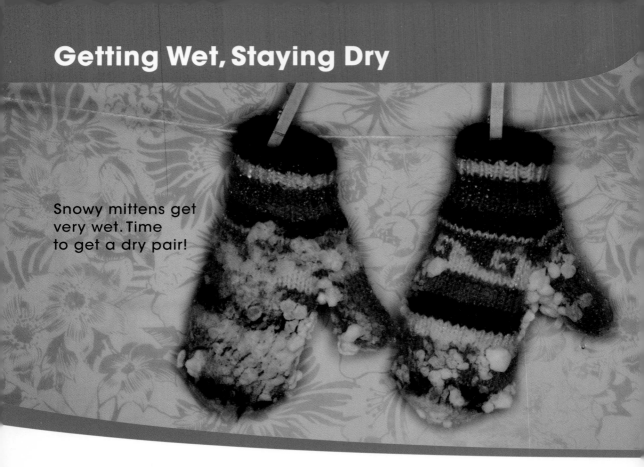

Snowy mittens get very wet. Time to get a dry pair!

It is morning at the campsite. It is starting to rain. What should you wear now?

Wool can get a little wet and still be pretty warm. Water beads up on top of the fabric. But if it rains hard or snows, wool gets very wet. Then it takes a long time to dry.

Cotton fibers soak up water. Water goes through cotton, too. That makes cotton very cold to wear in the rain.

Silk can get soaked in the rain. But it also absorbs sweat. It can keep hikers cool in warm weather. It also keeps people warm in cool weather. But it's not so good in the pouring rain.

What would *you* wear if you were camping in the rain?

Many companies add chemicals to fabrics. Polyester clothing has chemicals that keep water from soaking in.

What should your camping group wear if it rains a little? What if it rains a lot? Would your answer change if it were hot and raining? What about cold and raining?

Clothing Designer

Designers make clothes.
They know a lot about fabrics.
They want people to wear the clothes they design. The clothes need to look good and feel good to wear.

Each kind of fabric has its own look.
Silk is hard to clean. Cotton is easy to wash.
Which fabric do you think would be best for play clothes on a hot day?

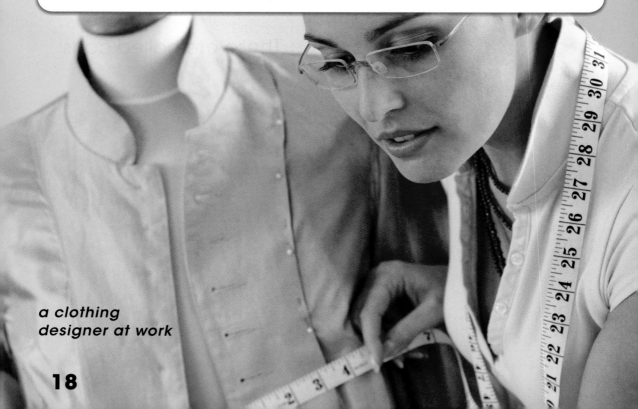

a clothing designer at work

cotton   wool

What to Wear?

What did you pack in your backpack? Here are reasons each fabric might be a good choice. These are called pros. There are also reasons each fabric might not be a perfect choice. These are called cons.

Fabric 1: Cotton

Pros: Cotton keeps you cool when it's sunny and warm.

Cons: It gets very wet and cold in the rain. It also gets wet when you sweat.

Fabric 2: Wool

Pros: Wool is very warm. It is OK to wear wool in a light rain.

Cons: Wool gets soaked in heavy rain. It can be thick and bulky to carry.

silk

polyester

Fabric 3: Silk

Pros: Silk is light and easy to carry. It keeps you warm when it's cold out. It keeps you cool when it's hot out.

Cons: Silk gets soaked in the rain. It is hard to clean.

Fabric 4: Polyester

Pros: Many types of this synthetic fabric keep you dry in the pouring rain.

Cons: Polyester might not let much air through. You could get too hot.

Can you think of yet another option for staying comfortable during your camping trip? You might want to see what the weather **forecast** is. That way, you will be prepared for the weather!

Beyond the Puzzle

Fabric can keep you warm, cool, and dry. What else can fabric do?

Try this. Put on cotton clothes. Run around until you get hot. Write down how you feel. Are your clothes wet with sweat? How long does it take for you to cool off? How long does it take for your clothes to dry?

Try the same thing in different fabrics. Wait a little while to cool down. Which fabrics worked best for running? Do you think other fabrics would be best for other sports? As you've learned, knowing about different types of fabrics can keep you comfortable whatever you are doing.

Glossary

cocoons: cases made by silkworms and other insects.

fabrics: cloth.

fibers: tiny threads.

flax: a plant used to make a fabric called linen.

forecast: a statement that something pertaining to weather will happen in the future, such as rain.

knitting: a way to tie yarn in little knots to make fabric.

polyester: a synthetic fabric.

silk: fabric made from the material spun by silkworms.

synthetic: made by humans, not in nature.

weave: to pass yarn strings under and over each other to make fabric.

wool: sheep hair; also the fabric and yarn made from sheep hair.

yarn: fibers twisted together; used in knitting or weaving.

Further Reading

How We Use Cotton, by Chris Oxlade. Heinemann-Raintree, 2005.

Silkworms, Martha E.H. Rustad, Pebble, 2009.

Wool, by Andrew Langley. Crabtree Publishing, 2008.

History for Kids. **History of Cotton.**
www.historyforkids.org/learn/clothing/cotton.htm

Additional Notes

The page references below provide answers to questions asked throughout the book. Questions whose answers will vary are not addressed.

Page 13: Caption question: There are two patterns.

Page 14: No. Cotton would be better for the day. Wool would be better for night.

Page 15: Silk would be good in situations that were warm and dry. Wool would be better in the cold and wet.

Page 17: Polyester would be best if it rains a little. Wool would be better if it rains a lot. Polyester might be best if it is hot and rainy. Wool would be the choice for a cold, rainy day.

Page 18: Cotton would be best for play clothes on a hot day.

Page 20: Another option is to wear many layers of clothing. That way you can take things off and put them back on depending on the changing weather or your changing activity level.

Page 21: Silk probably works best for running. Which fabric would be best would depend on the season and weather during which each sport took place.

Index